Lerner SPORTS ™

GREATEST OF ALL TIME TEAMS

G.O.A.T.
FOOTBALL TEAMS

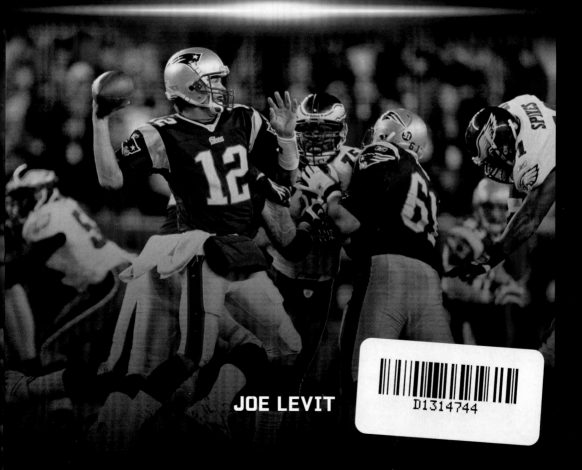

JOE LEVIT

D1314744

Lerner Publications ◆ Minneapolis

To Erik Federer, a best friend in football and in life

Lerner Publications Company
An imprint of Lerner Publishing Group, Inc.
241 First Avenue North
Minneapolis, MN 55401 USA
For reading levels and more information, look up this title at www.lernerbooks.com.

Main body text set in Aptifer Sans LT Pro.Typeface provided by Linotype AG.

Designer: Kimberly Morales **Lerner team:** Sue Marquis

Library of Congress Cataloging-in-Publication Data

Names: Levit, Joseph, author. | Lerner Publications Company.
Title: G.O.A.T. football teams / Joe Levit.
Other titles: Greatest of All Time football teams
Description: Minneapolis : Lerner Publications, 2021. | Series: Greatest of All Time Teams (Lerner Sports) | Includes bibliographical references and index. | Audience: Ages 7–11 years | Audience: Grades 2–3 | Summary: "From the undefeated 1972 Miami Dolphins to Tom Brady's best New England Patriots team, meet the greatest NFL teams of all time. The fun top-ten-list format is supported by plenty of fascinating facts and stats"— Provided by publisher.
Identifiers: LCCN 2020003637 (print) | LCCN 2020003638 (ebook) | ISBN 9781728404400 (Library Binding) | ISBN 9781728418230 (eBook)
Subjects: LCSH: Football teams—Records. | Football teams—United States—History—Juvenile literature. | American Football Conference—History—Juvenile literature. | National Football Conference—History—Juvenile literature. | Super Bowl—History—Juvenile literature. | National Football League—History—Juvenile literature.
Classification: LCC GV955 .L48 2021 (print) | LCC GV955 (ebook) | DDC 796.33202/02—dc23

LC record available at https://lccn.loc.gov/2020003637
LC ebook record available at https://lccn.loc.gov/2020003638

Manufactured in the United States of America
2-50933-49012-5/12/2021

TABLE OF CONTENTS

Patrick Mahomes led the Kansas City Chiefs to victory in the 2020 Super Bowl.

FOOTBALL'S GREATEST

Many great teams have played in the National Football League (NFL). But which teams are the greatest of all time (G.O.A.T.)? It's a fun question, but it doesn't have an easy answer.

FACTS AT A GLANCE

>> The 2007 New England Patriots went 18–0 before losing in the Super Bowl.

>> In 1999, the St. Louis Rams scored 526 points. The team's amazing offense was called the Greatest Show on Turf.

>> The Dallas Cowboys faced the Buffalo Bills in the 1993 Super Bowl. The Cowboys defense scored two touchdowns in a 52–17 victory.

>> The 1972 Miami Dolphins are the only NFL team to win all their games and the Super Bowl.

>> The 1985 Chicago Bears defense allowed only 198 points in the regular season. That was 65 fewer points allowed than the next best team.

In 1967, the Green Bay Packers and the Kansas City Chiefs played in the first Super Bowl. That season, the NFL had only 16 teams. By 2002, the league had doubled in size. How do you compare teams from the 1960s to recent teams?

The best teams of all time have a few things in common. They usually have several players in the Pro Football Hall of Fame. Each team was excellent at either offense or defense. Some were great at both.

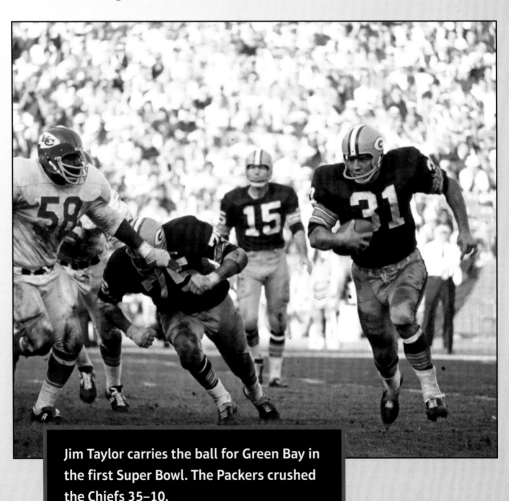

Jim Taylor carries the ball for Green Bay in the first Super Bowl. The Packers crushed the Chiefs 35–10.

New York Giants players celebrate a touchdown in the 2012 Super Bowl. The Giants have won four Super Bowls, but none of those teams are the G.O.A.T.

You may not know some of the teams in this book. But it's impossible to tell the history of the NFL without them. You might disagree with how the teams are ranked, or you might feel that one of the best teams was left out. Your friends will have their own opinions about the G.O.A.T. teams too. That's okay. It's part of the fun. Learning about the NFL's greatest teams and thinking about the rankings are what this book is all about.

Randy Moss catches a long pass in 2007.

NO. 10 2007 NEW ENGLAND PATRIOTS

In 2007, the Patriots were close to perfect. To help superstar quarterback Tom Brady, the team added three top wide receivers before the season started. Randy Moss, Wes Welker, and Donté Stallworth helped give New England one of the best offenses in league history.

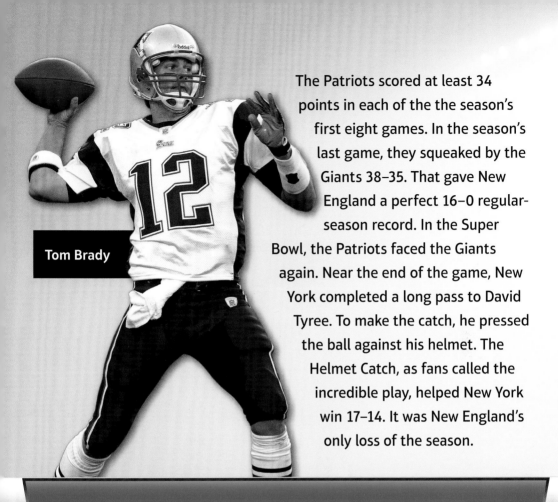

Tom Brady

The Patriots scored at least 34 points in each of the the season's first eight games. In the season's last game, they squeaked by the Giants 38–35. That gave New England a perfect 16–0 regular-season record. In the Super Bowl, the Patriots faced the Giants again. Near the end of the game, New York completed a long pass to David Tyree. To make the catch, he pressed the ball against his helmet. The Helmet Catch, as fans called the incredible play, helped New York win 17–14. It was New England's only loss of the season.

2007 PATRIOTS STATS

>>> Tom Brady passed for 50 touchdowns, setting a single-season record.

>>> Randy Moss set an NFL record with 23 touchdown catches.

>>> The offense set an NFL record by scoring 314 points during road games.

>>> The Patriots outscored their opponents by 315 points, the biggest difference in NFL history.

>>> New England's defense racked up 47 sacks, second most in the NFL.

Seattle Seahawks defenders swarm around an opposing player and drag him to the ground.

9

2013 SEATTLE SEAHAWKS

The 2013 Seattle Seahawks were stacked with talent. Leading the attack were running back Marshawn Lynch and quarterback Russell Wilson. On defense, the team had a strong group of superstars. But the defensive backs stole the show. Nicknamed the Legion of Boom, the group made big hits and big plays. They led the team to a 13–3 regular season record.

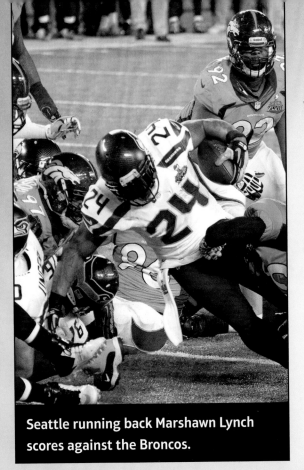
Seattle running back Marshawn Lynch scores against the Broncos.

The Super Bowl that season was a clash of styles. The powerful Seahawks defense faced Peyton Manning and the top-scoring Denver Broncos offense. Denver had topped 50 points in a game three times during the season. But in the Super Bowl, the Seahawks shut down Manning. Seattle recorded a safety 12 seconds into the game. No team had ever scored so quickly in a Super Bowl. The Seahawks buried the Broncos 43–8.

2013 SEAHAWKS STATS

- ▶▶▶ Seattle's defense had a league-leading 28 interceptions.
- ▶▶▶ The defense ranked first in yards allowed per game (274).
- ▶▶▶ The Seahawks allowed the fewest points per game (14).
- ▶▶▶ The defense led the league in points allowed (231), yards allowed (4,378), and takeaways (39).
- ▶▶▶ The team outscored their opponents by 186 points.

Kurt Warner was one of the most accurate passers in the NFL.

NO. 8

1999 ST. LOUIS RAMS

Nicknamed the Greatest Show on Turf, the 1999 St. Louis Rams stunned opposing teams. They put up points at a pace few could match. The Rams went 13–3 in the regular season. With the help of receivers Torry Holt and Isaac Bruce, quarterback Kurt Warner threw 41 touchdowns. Offensive lineman Orlando Pace smashed defenders. Warner, Pace, and running back Marshall Faulk are all in

St. Louis needed all their scoring power in the playoffs against the Minnesota Vikings. The Rams outscored Minnesota 49–37. Then the Rams defense shut down the Tampa Bay Buccaneers in an 11–6 victory. St. Louis faced the Tennessee Titans in the Super Bowl. On the last play of the game, St. Louis defender Mike Jones tackled Kevin Dyson at the one-yard line. Jones stopped Dyson from scoring and secured the 23–16 win for St. Louis.

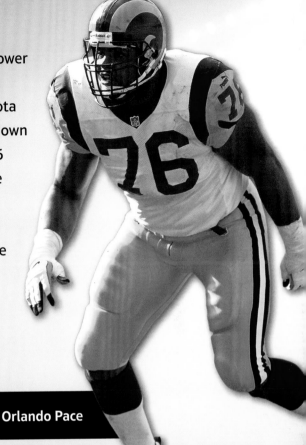

Orlando Pace

1999 RAMS STATS

⟫⟫⟫ The Rams averaged almost 33 points per game.

⟫⟫⟫ St. Louis led the league with 526 points scored.

⟫⟫⟫ Marshall Faulk racked up over 1,000 yards rushing and 1,000 yards receiving.

⟫⟫⟫ The Rams defense totaled 57 sacks, tied for the league lead.

⟫⟫⟫ The defense scored eight touchdowns.

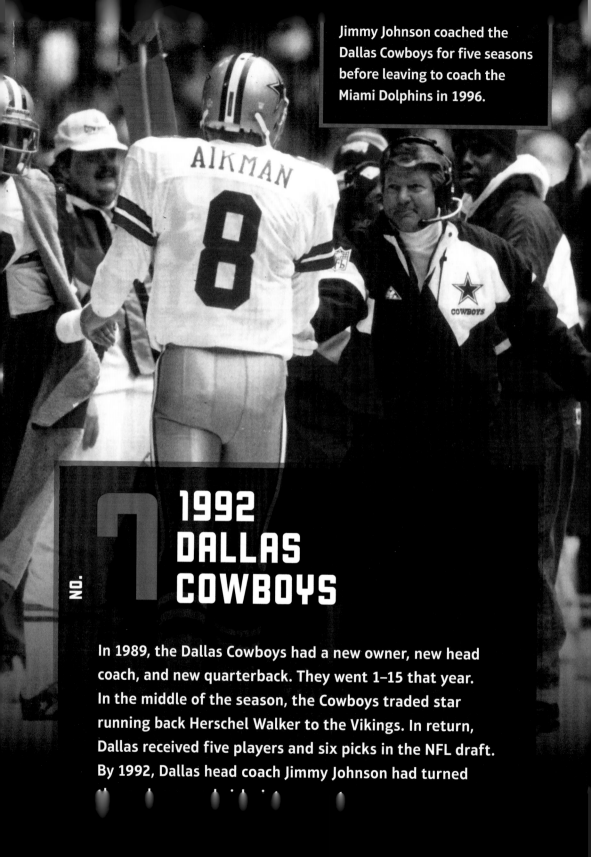

Jimmy Johnson coached the Dallas Cowboys for five seasons before leaving to coach the Miami Dolphins in 1996.

1992
DALLAS
COWBOYS

In 1989, the Dallas Cowboys had a new owner, new head coach, and new quarterback. They went 1–15 that year. In the middle of the season, the Cowboys traded star running back Herschel Walker to the Vikings. In return, Dallas received five players and six picks in the NFL draft. By 1992, Dallas head coach Jimmy Johnson had turned

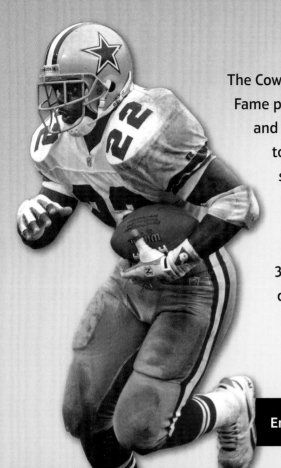

The Cowboys offense had future Hall-of-Fame players Troy Aikman, Emmitt Smith, and Michael Irvin. The team also played tough defense. After a 13–3 regular season, the Cowboys stormed through the playoffs. They crushed the Philadelphia Eagles 34–10. Then they beat the San Francisco 49ers 30–20. In the Super Bowl, Dallas destroyed the Bills 52–17!

Emmitt Smith

1992 COWBOYS STATS

>>> Emmitt Smith rushed for 1,713 yards to lead the NFL.

>>> Smith also led the league with 18 rushing touchdowns.

>>> The Dallas defense finished first in the NFL in yards allowed (3,931).

>>> In one game, the Cowboys held the Seattle Seahawks to only 62 yards of total offense.

>>> The Dallas defense scored two touchdowns in the Super Bowl.

Pittsburgh's Jack Lambert lowers his shoulders for a big hit.

NO. 6

1978 PITTSBURGH STEELERS

In the 1970s, the Pittsburgh Steelers defense was known as the Steel Curtain. By 1978, their offense was as good as their defense. The 1978 NFL season was the first with a 16-game schedule. The Steelers posted a 14–2 record, the

The Steelers pounded the Broncos 33–10 in the first game of the playoffs. In the next game, Pittsburgh forced nine turnovers against the Houston Oilers. The Steelers pumped Houston out of the playoffs 34–5. Next up was a Super Bowl battle with the defending champions, the Cowboys. Pittsburgh's offense carried the team to victory. Quarterback Terry Bradshaw had four passing touchdowns, including two to John Stallworth and one to Lynn Swann. Both Stallworth and Swann had over 100 receiving yards. The Steelers held on for a 35–31 win.

Terry Bradshaw

1978 STEELERS STATS

- The Pittsburgh defense tied for second in the NFL with 48 turnovers.
- The Steelers defense allowed just over 12 points per game, the fewest in the league.
- Pittsburgh's defense led the NFL with 195 points allowed.
- Terry Bradshaw's 28 passing touchdowns led the league.
- The Steelers had 12 players voted best in the league at their position.

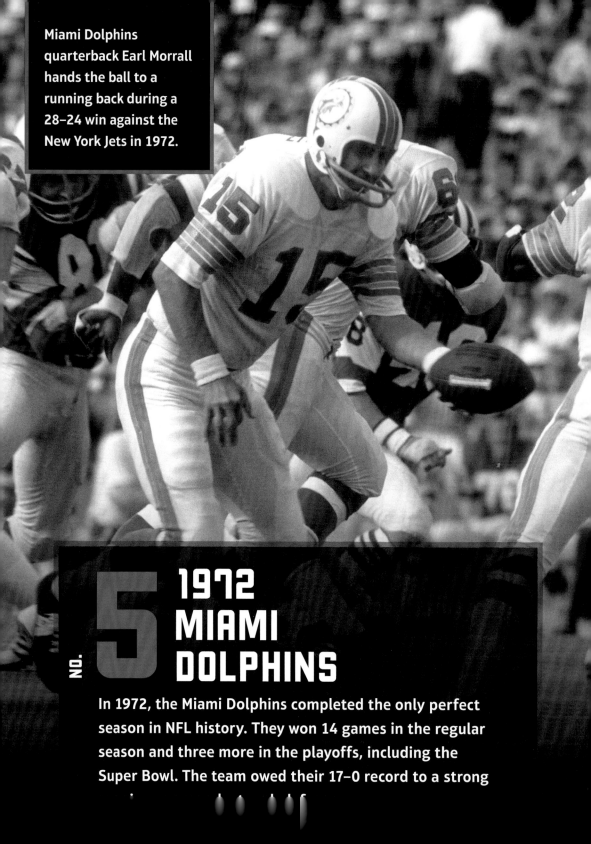

Miami Dolphins quarterback Earl Morrall hands the ball to a running back during a 28–24 win against the New York Jets in 1972.

NO. 5

1972 MIAMI DOLPHINS

In 1972, the Miami Dolphins completed the only perfect season in NFL history. They won 14 games in the regular season and three more in the playoffs, including the Super Bowl. The team owed their 17–0 record to a strong

That season, running backs Larry Csonka and Mercury Morris both rushed for 1,000 yards or more. Miami's third runner, Jim Kiick, had 521 yards. Kiick's total would have led three other NFL teams. The Dolphins also had the best defense in football. They didn't have many superstars, but the players worked well together. In the Super Bowl, the Dolphins topped the Washington Redskins 14–7.

Mercury Morris

1972 DOLPHINS STATS

▶▶▶ Larry Csonka and Mercury Morris were the first teammates in NFL history to rush for 1,000 or more yards.

▶▶▶ The Dolphins led the NFL in points scored (385).

▶▶▶ They led the league in yards gained (5,036).

▶▶▶ The Miami defense allowed the league's fewest yards gained (3,297).

▶▶▶ The defense allowed the fewest points in the NFL (171).

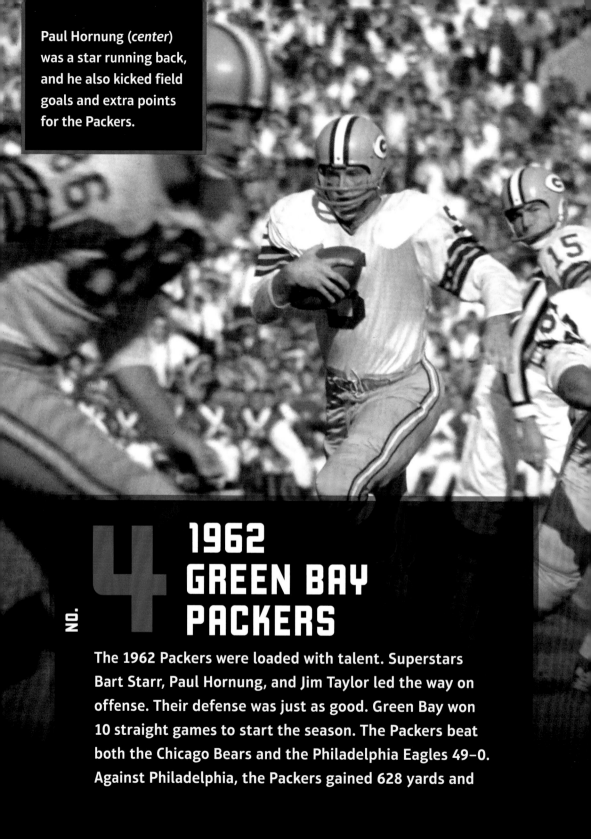

Paul Hornung (*center*) was a star running back, and he also kicked field goals and extra points for the Packers.

NO. 4
1962 GREEN BAY PACKERS

The 1962 Packers were loaded with talent. Superstars Bart Starr, Paul Hornung, and Jim Taylor led the way on offense. Their defense was just as good. Green Bay won 10 straight games to start the season. The Packers beat both the Chicago Bears and the Philadelphia Eagles 49–0. Against Philadelphia, the Packers gained 628 yards and

Bart Starr (*center*) played for the Packers from 1956 to 1971.

The only team to give the Packers trouble that year was the Detroit Lions. In Green Bay, the Packers snuck by Detroit 9–7 on three Hornung field goals. But the Lions got revenge. They beat Green Bay 26–14 in Detroit on Thanksgiving. The NFL championship game was at Yankee Stadium in New York on a chilly day. The Packers beat the Giants 16–7. Green Bay finished the season 14–1.

1962 PACKERS STATS

>>> The Packers led the NFL in points scored (415) and points allowed (148).

>>> Green Bay scored 36 rushing touchdowns, setting the single-season record.

>>> Running back Jim Taylor had 1,474 rushing yards and 19 touchdowns.

>>> The Packers defense led the league with 50 turnovers.

>>> The defense led the NFL in interceptions (31) and passing yards allowed (1,746).

Joe Montana won four Super Bowls with the San Francisco 49ers.

1989
SAN FRANCISCO
49ERS

The 1989 San Francisco 49ers had a powerful offense. They were a great passing team, leading the league with more than 8 yards gained per pass attempt. It helped that the 49ers had two future Hall-of-Fame quarterbacks, Joe Montana and Steve Young. Montana threw 26 touchdowns and ran in three more. Montana missed three games due to injury. Young stepped in, and the team kept rolling.

Jerry Rice celebrates a touchdown with his teammates.

After a 14–2 regular season, the 49ers played even better in the playoffs. They crushed the Vikings 41–13. Then they faced the Los Angeles Rams. The Rams were one of two teams that had beaten San Francisco in the regular season. But this time, the 49ers took them down 30–3. In the Super Bowl, San Francisco faced the Broncos. Denver had the league's best defense. They'd allowed just 226 points in the regular season. But they were no match for San Francisco. The 49ers destroyed the Broncos 55–10!

1989 49ERS STATS

>>> Wide receivers Jerry Rice and John Taylor each racked up more than 1,000 receiving yards.

>>> Rice caught 17 touchdowns, and Taylor caught 10.

>>> Running back Roger Craig rushed for over 1,000 yards.

>>> In three playoff games, Montana had 800 passing yards, 11 touchdowns, and no interceptions.

>>> The defense ranked third in the NFL in points allowed (253).

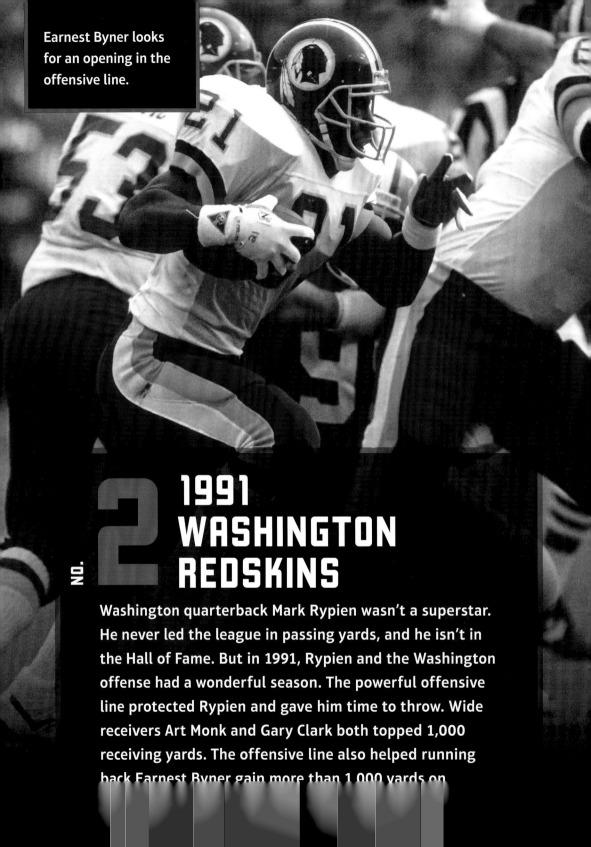

Earnest Byner looks for an opening in the offensive line.

2

1991 WASHINGTON REDSKINS

Washington quarterback Mark Rypien wasn't a superstar. He never led the league in passing yards, and he isn't in the Hall of Fame. But in 1991, Rypien and the Washington offense had a wonderful season. The powerful offensive line protected Rypien and gave him time to throw. Wide receivers Art Monk and Gary Clark both topped 1,000 receiving yards. The offensive line also helped running back Earnest Byner gain more than 1,000 yards on

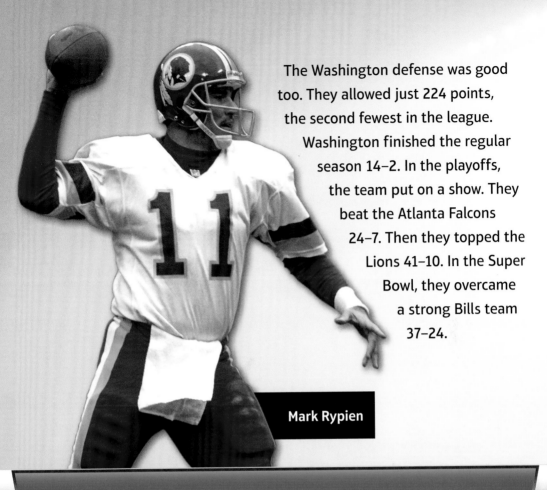

The Washington defense was good too. They allowed just 224 points, the second fewest in the league. Washington finished the regular season 14–2. In the playoffs, the team put on a show. They beat the Atlanta Falcons 24–7. Then they topped the Lions 41–10. In the Super Bowl, they overcame a strong Bills team 37–24.

Mark Rypien

1991 WASHINGTON STATS

▶▶▶ Washington led the league in points scored (485).

▶▶▶ The Washington offense led the NFL with about 8 yards gained per pass attempt. The defense allowed just under 5 yards per pass attempt, second best in the league.

▶▶▶ Backup running back Ricky Ervins ran for 680 yards. That would have led nine other NFL teams.

▶▶▶ Washington allowed only nine sacks all year, the fewest in the league. Washington's 50 sacks of opposing quarterbacks was tied for third.

▶▶▶ The Washington defense forced 41 turnovers and allowed just 224 points.

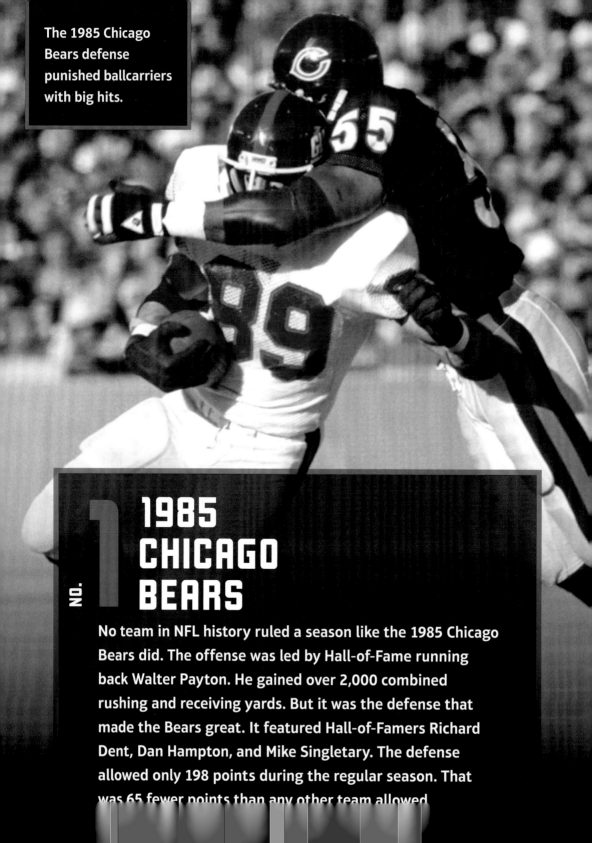

The 1985 Chicago Bears defense punished ballcarriers with big hits.

1985 CHICAGO BEARS

No team in NFL history ruled a season like the 1985 Chicago Bears did. The offense was led by Hall-of-Fame running back Walter Payton. He gained over 2,000 combined rushing and receiving yards. But it was the defense that made the Bears great. It featured Hall-of-Famers Richard Dent, Dan Hampton, and Mike Singletary. The defense allowed only 198 points during the regular season. That was 65 fewer points than any other team allowed.

The Bears finished the regular season 15–1. In the playoffs, they completely crushed the competition. The defense didn't allow a single point against them in the first two games. In the Super Bowl, they overpowered the Patriots 46–10. In three playoff games, the Bears outscored their opponents 91–10. The incredible offense and defense of the 1985 Chicago Bears make them the greatest team of all time.

Walter Payton

1985 BEARS STATS

>>> The Bears scored 456 points and allowed only 198.

>>> The Chicago offense finished first in the NFL in rushing yards (2,761).

>>> The defense had 64 sacks, the most ever for a Super Bowl–winning team.

>>> The defense led the league with 34 interceptions.

>>> The defense led the league in yards allowed (4,135) and takeaways (54).

YOUR
G.O.A.T.

Think about the rankings in this book, and then check out the Learn More section on page 31. You'll find books and websites with information about great football teams of the past and present. Read about some of the terrific teams that didn't make the cut in this book, such as the 1998 Denver Broncos and the 1976 Oakland Raiders.

Search online for more information. Or check with a librarian, who may have other resources for you to discover. You might even reach out to NFL coaches or teams on social media to see what they think.

Once you're ready, make your list of the greatest teams of all time. Then ask your friends to make their own lists and compare them. Do you have teams listed that no one else has? Are you missing a team that your friends thought was sure to be on the list? Discuss the results, and try to impress people with your choices!

FOOTBALL FACTS

▶▶▶ The Dallas Cowboys are the NFL's most valuable team, according to *Forbes* magazine. The Cowboys top the list with a value of $5 billion.

▶▶▶ Dallas isn't just the most valuable NFL team. They're the most valuable sports team in the world. Their value puts them just ahead of baseball's New York Yankees and the soccer team Real Madrid.

▶▶▶ The largest margin of victory between two NFL teams occurred when the Chicago Bears beat the Washington Redskins 73–0 in the 1940 championship game.

▶▶▶ In 2017, the New England Patriots set a Super Bowl record for the biggest comeback. Trailing the Atlanta Falcons 28–3 in the second half, the Patriots came back to win 34–28 in overtime.

▶▶▶ In 2018, Tennessee Titans running back Derrick Henry ran the ball from his own 1-yard line. He raced up the sideline, pushing defenders out of the way to score a 99-yard touchdown. It was just the second 99-yard rushing score in NFL history.

GLOSSARY

defensive back: a player whose main job is to defend passes

draft: an event where teams take turns choosing new players

field goal: a score of three points made by kicking the ball over the crossbar

interception: when a defensive player catches a pass intended for an offensive player

offensive line: the five players on the offensive side of the line of scrimmage who block defenders

Pro Football Hall of Fame: a building in Canton, Ohio, housing memorials to the greatest football players of all time

regular season: games played by all the teams in the NFL to determine which teams will make the playoffs

sack: tackle the quarterback behind the line of scrimmage

safety: a play in which a member of the offensive team is tackled behind its own goal line that counts two points for the defensive team

turnover: when the offense loses the ball because the defense recovers a fumble or intercepts a pass

LEARN MORE

Cooper, Robert. *The Pro Football Hall of Fame*. Minneapolis: Pop!, 2020.

Jacobs, Greg. *The Everything Kids' Football Book: All-Time Greats, Legendary Teams, and Today's Favorite Players—with Tips on Playing like a Pro*. Avon, MA: Adams Media, 2018.

Levit, Joe. *Football's G.O.A.T. Jim Brown, Tom Brady, and More*. Minneapolis: Lerner Publications, 2020.

NFL 100
https://www.nfl.com/100/originals/100-greatest/browse-videos

Pro Football Hall of Fame
https://www.profootballhof.com/

Sports Illustrated Kids—Football
https://www.sikids.com/football

INDEX

PHOTO ACKNOWLEDGMENTS

Image credits: Drew Hallowell/Getty Images, p. 1; Jamie Squire/Getty Images, p. 4; Flores/Getty Images, p. 6; Jim Davis/The Boston Globe/Getty Images, p. 7; Ron Antonelli/New York Daily News Archive/Getty Images, p. 8; Stephen Dunn/ Getty Images, p. 9; Al Bello/Getty Images, pp. 10, 13; Focus on Sport/Getty Images, pp. 11, 12, 17, 18, 19, 20, 25, 27; Joseph Patronite/Getty Images, p. 14; Peter Brouillet/Getty Images, p. 15; George Gojkovich/Getty Images, p. 16; AP Photo/NFL Photos, p. 21; AP Photo/Tom DiPace, p. 22; AP Photo/John Gapps III, p. 23; George Rose/Getty Images, p. 24; Ronald C. Modra/Getty Images, p. 26; Mtsaride/Shutterstock.com, p. 28 (football). Design elements: ESB Professional/ Shutterstock.com; RaiDztor/Shutterstock.com; EFKS/Shutterstock.com; Vitalii Kozyrskyi/Shutterstock.com; Roman Sotola/Shutterstock.com; MEandMO/ Shutterstock.com.

Cover: Drew Hallowell/Getty Images. Design elements: RaiDztor/Shutterstock. com; MIKHAIL GRACHIKOV/Shutterstock.com; ijaydesign99/Shutterstock.com.